POLICE CARS

POLICE CARS

IAN KERR

CHARTWELL
BOOKS, INC.

This edition published in 1998 by
CHARTWELL BOOKS, INC.
A division of BOOK SALES, INC
114 Northfield Avenue,
Edison, New Jersey 08837

Produced by
PRC Publishing Ltd,
Kiln House, 210 New Kings Road, London SW6 4NZ

ISBN 0 78580 948 1

Printed and bound in China

Dedication

To Mum and Dad

Acknowledgements

The photographs, unless specifically credited, were taken by Simon Clay.

CONTENTS

INTRODUCTION

Right: A line up of New York's finest, ready for action.

Many people, at some stage in their lives, will have considered becoming a police officer. The desire, however fleeting, will probably have been elicited by the sight of a police vehicle speeding through traffic or down an open highway on the way to an incident. It is the perception of adventure and the excitement of such high-speed runs, with lights flashing and sirens sounding, that is the main stimulus—something reinforced by the way the police are portrayed on television. Our image of policework through the media almost always concentrates on the thrills and excitement of the job, highlighting the car chases and ignoring the tedium!

Sitting in an office, or stuck in a traffic jam, the sound of sirens piercing the air always attracts our attention—as do the flashing lights as they bounce and strobe off windows—and we try to work out from where the vehicle is coming.

On the open road flashing lights in the rear-view mirror always grab your attention. After the initial heart-stopping moment of guilt as you check your speed and realize you cannot possibly be the culprit, you wait to see the vehicle pass to identify which of the emergency services is involved.

If it's the fire service or an ambulance there is an automatic assumption of the type of incident involved, but with the police it is different: the possible scenarios are just too varied to be able to guess at—the unit could be responding to anything from a road accident to a shoot-out.

In reality, wherever it is heading, the police car is just a tool to get the officer to the scene. What we see as glamorous high-speed driving is just part of the job and the vehicle must be equipped to cope with whatever is required of it. Above all, it has to be safe, capable of high speeds, and able to cope with stopping repeatedly from these speeds. It must be comfortable for the driver, who has to spend many hours in it, and it must be capable of housing all the sophisticated modern weapons used in the fight against crime.

Of course, there are other types of police car, specialized back-up vehicles that do not patrol as a general rule, but are brought out as needs arise: but these are very different beasts to the general patrol car. This basic police vehicle has got to be capable of imposing its presence on the scene of any incident—from minor, run-of-the-mill, daily occurrences to the rare major crimes. The car must be psychologically superior in appearance, so that everybody recognizes it and its occupants as authoritative—because of this, as much as anything, only certain vehicles are deemed suitable for the role. Vigorous testing of their construction and performance identifies the relatively small number of vehicle types capable of doing the job—in many cases police specification versions of the manufacturers' standard ranges.

This also means that police cars all over the country are of a very similar, if not the same, type and often differ only because they bear the different markings and insignia of the various police authorities.

This book aims to show just some of the many marked vehicles in use throughout the United States—vehicles that run 24 hours a day, 365 days a year. It highlights the main types and, because the subject is so large, only briefly examines specialized vehicles and unmarked, covert, cars—if you want to see the latter look in any parking lot: any vehicle there could be an undercover police car.

One thing is certain, however: whether unmarked or marked, old or new, it will have been carefully tested and meticulously maintained—the police car has to perform a very varied job and it has to be maintained in a condition to perform it.

HISTORY

In the early days, there was little need for peace-keeping officers to have any form of transport because there was so little in the way of significant population movement. Crime was usually contained within the local area, committed by local inhabitants, and more often than not the criminals were well known to everybody.

As time progressed, personal mobility increased, allowing the criminal to move more easily from one place to another—at first by horse and then by some system of mechanical transport, mainly the train. As a result, those charged with keeping the peace and maintaining law and order had to be able to follow suit.

8

Below right: As the new century moved into top gear, vehicles were becoming a more common sight on the mostly dirt-based roads, although there were no police specials. Here we see members of the Los Angeles Police Department with an open top tourer used as transport. *Archive Photos/American stock*

Far Right: New York police at the same time were, however, still mainly on foot, with the odd horse still in service as this photograph of a parade in 1897 shows. *Archive Photos/Museum of the City of New York*

At the turn of the century the development of the internal combustion engine meant that personal motorized transport became available. As this developed and the prices dropped, more and more people had access to it, and the ability to cover far greater distances in a much shorter time became commonplace. Despite improved methods of communication by such means as the telegraph, there was still a need for law enforcement officers to travel after their quarry and the railroad was not always the quickest or most practical method of pursuit.

The motorcycle was the first main form of motorized transport adopted in numbers by lawmen. Bikes were more akin to horses, cheaper and more readily available than cars. However, motorcycles could only carry one person at the time—which left nowhere to put an arrested outlaw! It was this need that led to the introduction of trucks and some of the larger cars on the market to transport

951 THE WEST COAST ART CO., LOS ANGELES, C.

Right: New York Police had caught the four-wheeled bug by the time the 1920s started. This is a two-seater coupe from the 7th Precinct. Although the word "Police" is along the folding bonnet sides complementing the side markings, there is nothing to identify the vehicle in the mirror, just an alley light on the driver's side and some horns at the front. *Archive Photos*

Far Right: This 1935 Ford did duty in Colorado and has been restored to its original livery. Note the alley light already coming into being on the driver's side and the small "Mickey Mouse" red lights on the top instead of one main light unit.

Below: After World War 2 the car was firmly established with police specials being offered by the factories. Here a Kentucky State Police trooper waits for an offender.

Far Right: New York in the 1950s reflected the huge growth of car use with a large population and a growing number of vehicles. The police department had embraced the car as a necessary evil and had a mixed fleet of cars. Pictured is a Plymouth with an illuminated police sign above the windshield.

Right: The bad guys were also using cars—as getaway vehicles—and the police had to make use of their biggest advantage, the radio, to set up roadblocks rather than just chasing the miscreants. Here the police in the city of Rye appear to have used at least one of these cars before in a similar situation! *Archive Photos*

Below Right: This Chevrolet shows a customary lack of markings (see also the vehicles above), apart from those on the doors. In use by the Ohio Turnpike Patrol in 1955, it does have a massive light unit on the top which must have weighed a ton and done nothing for the aerodynamics! *Archive Photos*

squads of officers to the scene of a disturbance. Whilst many of these vehicles were indistinguishable from other vehicles on the road, they gained the name "squad" cars after their carrying abilities.

Throughout the country, the law enforcement agencies used straightforward ordinary vehicles. There was no special significance in the police vehicle at this time, although manufacturers were quick on the uptake. Many of the major car producers started making police specials specifically

Above: No real worries regarding the weight of the light unit on this V8 Dodge in use in Indiana. The state police officer is pictured using the radio in 1957. *Archive Photos*

Right: Rhode Island State Police two years on, showing a more normal center-roof rotating-light on this Dodge. *Archive Photos*

Below Right: At the start of the swinging 1960s the police also started to brighten up: this New York patrol car from the Safety Unit sports a two-tone color scheme. Note the vehicle number and the bar light in addition to the center-mounted light, although all light units are still plain red. *Archive Photos*

Right: Pictured sitting by an intersection is a Chrysler police special—the 1960 "Enforcer," a very popular vehicle which saw use with law enforcement agencies throughout the United States during the 1950s and early 1960s. *Archive Photos*

for the law enforcement agencies. These vehicles had everything from tuned motors right through to armor-plating, bulletproof glass, and machine gun ports, especially during Prohibition.

As mobility became more and more important and a greater number of people had access to vehicles, so a new phenomenon appeared: the road traffic accident. People were getting killed and, as a result, traffic laws were introduced. To enforce these, the state highway patrols were

formed. Some were brought into being as early as the start of the 1920s, although most seem to have their origins in the late 1920s and early 1930s.

These laws were more responsible for the increased number and use of police vehicles (due to the size of the areas and length of roads they patroled), than anything else and the manufacturers started taking even more note of the needs of police. On top of this, those who controled the police purse strings recognized that, by using

Right: As compared to the two-tone New York patrol car on page 18, this 1963 Dodge in use by Landsdale officers is in a single plain color with just a solitary roof mounted light. Each agency did and still does their own thing. *Lambert/ Archive Photos*

Right: Close-up of the door markings of the Lansdale 1963 Dodge, also showing the vehicle number for ID purposes. *Lambert/Archive Photos*

Far Right: Concern over the environment is nothing new. Here a New Jersey patrolman examines the discharge into the air from chimneys in Perth Amboy during 1964. *Archive Photos*

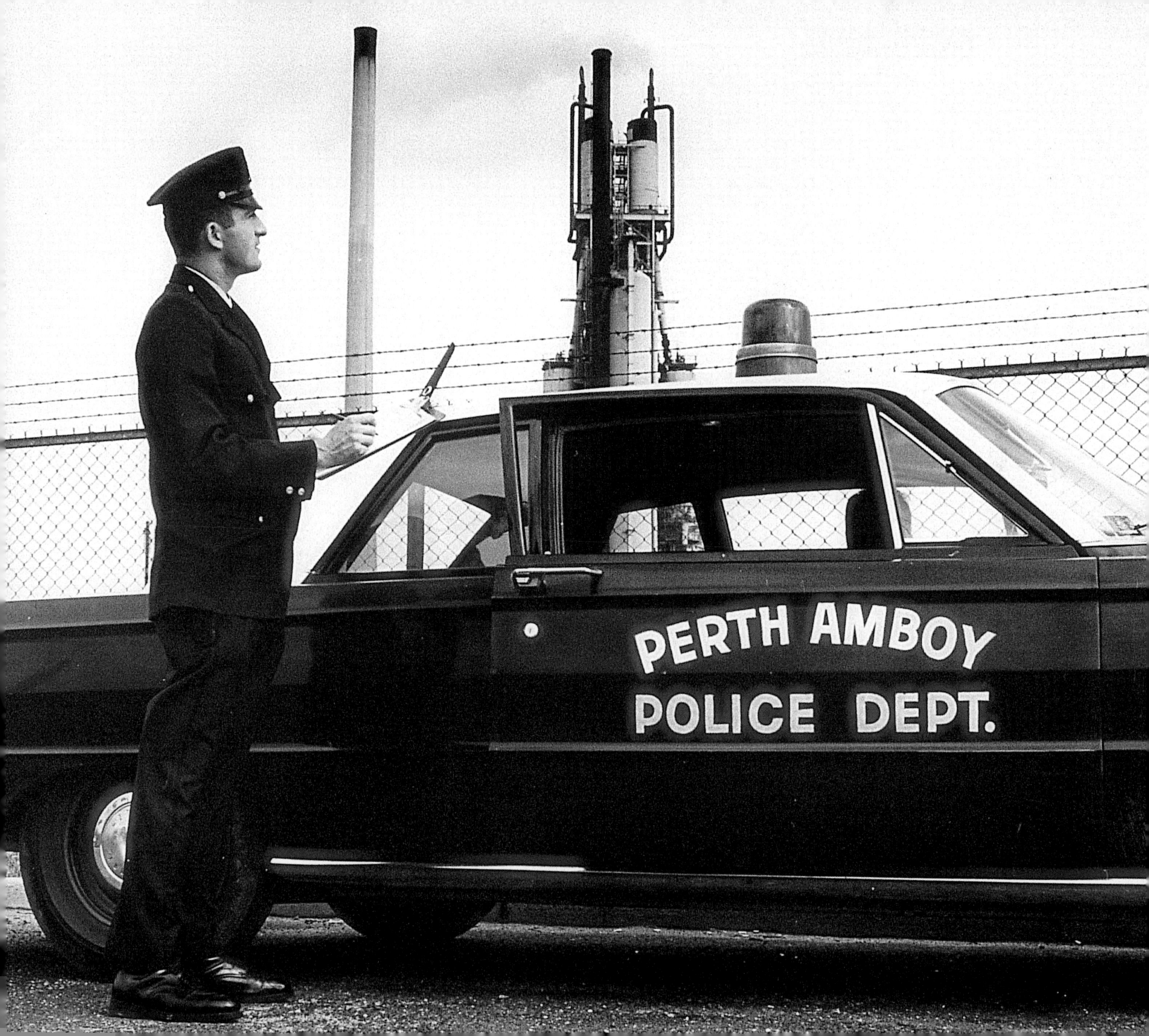
PERTH AMBOY
POLICE DEPT.

Far Right: The car is not always ideal for patroling in large cities or congested areas, so two wheels have always been part of the vehicle fleet. However, while many tend to think that single-track vehicles mean Harleys (or Indians before they went out of business) these two shots from Los Angeles and New York show the weather protection afforded by scooters; their light weight has also made them popular police patrol vehicles. *Archive Photos*

Right: Three wheels have also featured in police use. This shot shows a Harley Trike doing traffic duty in Los Angeles, just one of the police forces that made use of the extra carrying capacity of these strange three wheelers that also saw service as ice cream wagons! *Archive Photos*

vehicles with radios, greater areas could be policed by fewer people, allowing manpower savings. Detroit police had fitted a radio to a Ford Model T touring version as early as 1921. Other police departments soon learned of this and the effect it had on efficiency, and quickly followed suit.

At this time police cars began to be provided with equipment that differed from that of standard cars and was more specific to the roles they had to play. Vehicles gained specific markings that

identified them from other vehicles; red lights (derived from tail lights) started to be used to warn of approach and of danger at the scene of an incident.

There were no standard markings then, however, and there are none even to this day. Not only in the United States, but all over the world, every police agency or force does its own thing with regard to crests, stripes, lights, and positioning of markings. The methodology may be different but the aim is always the same: to ensure that

Right: By the mid-1960s the New York City Police Department had moved to a blue and white color scheme with roof-mounted bar lights. Pictured here is an early Chevrolet parked next to a newer model out on the mean streets! *Ken Young*

Far Right: Another 1960s view—here a Plymouth of the NYPD. *Archive Photos*

everyone is left in no doubt that the vehicle is official, belongs to the police, and that people should respond accordingly!

As with markings, the development of the police car itself was slow until the start of the 1950s, by which time vehicles were being used by virtually every law enforcement agency. They had to be, to police the huge number of vehicles on the roads. Cars featured in nearly every type of crime, even if just as a getaway vehicle. The police had to respond to this increase, and so did the manufacturers.

With this increase in market potential, the large manufacturers started producing police specials in earnest. Many cars gained high performance motors beneath the hood, although manufacturers stopped short of fitting the most powerful motors, worried no doubt that the rest of the car would not be able to cope, or that the engine itself would not stand constant daily use. Of course, there was also the cost factor, something that grew in importance over the years. The car makers had a number of important parameters to get right to produce an

Left: By the 1970s the NYPD's blue and white color scheme was a well established and familiar sight. *Archive Photos*

Above: Montgomery County, MA, Sheriff's office on the other hand still relies on the sheriff's star motif to identify their vehicles. This shot shows a plain marking scheme relying mainly on the light bars for its idenitification. *Ken Young*

Right: Still in New York State, but Nassau County has different ideas of vehicle marking to the New York City police. Interestingly the roof is painted red considering a single red light is used!
Archive Photos

efficient police car: they had to be reliable to meet the stringent requirements of constant use—often meaning that components such as brakes, suspension, etc., had to be uprated—while still being reasonably fuel efficient and comfortable, as well as affordable! With the introduction of modern technology, other requirements became necessary. The cars had to be able to carry sophisticated computers and other electrical gadgetry—hence most run today with uprated alternators to keep the lights, computers, and air conditioning running even at tick-over.

Why hasn't a manufacturer grasped the bull by the horns and produced a specific, customized police car instead of adapting standard production cars to meet police needs? It's a difficult question to answer considering the size of police motor fleets. However, despite what you may regard as the unfavorably large amount of police vehicles on the road, the actual number purchased each year is, in reality, very small in relation to the manufacturing costs—so it is likely that the unit cost of this perfect vehicle would be considerably greater than the current vehicles.

And would it be so perfect? To produce a customized police vehicle would involve a gigantic investment, and there would be considerable practical difficulties in terms of standardization: all the various agencies would want different items as standard, some counteracting others, so it would be impractical. Of course, additionally, there would then be no guarantee that everyone would buy the specially made car.

So, while all police cars have similar requirements, nevertheless standard vehicles are used—and so the evolution of the police car is as complicated and diverse as that of the motor industry itself. Coupled with the evolution of law enforcement and peace-keeping, this means we can only scratch the surface of the subject of police cars in a book of this kind. For those who wish to dig deeper, there are many other specialized books; we hope in the following pages to give a broad view of police cars in the United States and insight into the fascinatingly varied world of police vehicles.

Vehicle Types

Below: An impressive line up of Mustangs and their drivers. Alabama state troopers believe most strongly in discouraging fast driving on their roads.

Right: Utah Highway Patrol vehicles use several different vehicles. Seen here are just three: a Chevrolet Camaro, a Ford Taurus, and a Ford Mustang.

The life of a police car is not an easy one. In many cases what started life on the drawing board intended to be just another family-sized saloon ends up being loaded up like an estate car and driven like a sports car. The vehicle is expected to excel in all of these roles. The engine must be able to run at high speed, sit and idle for long periods and not overheat, and not be off the road for long periods due to mechanical breakdown. While it may have a few adaptations to help it do all of these things, it is, nevertheless, just a variant of a production vehicle.

As we have already discussed, no vehicle manufacturer creates a car specifically for the law enforcement market: they just adapt existing vehicles to the individual police department's specific requirements, born out of experience and testing. It is for these basic reasons that most cars up and down the country are the same, differing only in the livery and the equipment fitted. Today there are three main manufacturers supplying the bulk of these vehicles: Ford, Chevrolet, and Dodge. We shall examine them individually.

Ford

Ford is one of the biggest suppliers of police vehicles throughout the world. It was one of, if not the first, to supply specific police packages and adaptations of mainstream Ford production vehicles. In 1932 the company produced a police special using its then all-new V-8 engine. So successful was this, that it lasted right through to the early 1950s powering police specials. Nowadays, however, Ford produces several vehicles for police use.

Mustang
The Ford Mustang came into being as a police vehicle back in the 1980s, with the California Highway Patrol being the first to use the vehicle as a performance car. Mustangs were touted as being able to catch other performance vehicles thanks to the use of the 302cu in motor beneath the long bonnet.

The motor is claimed to produce some 205hp at 4,200 rpm, but also has a massive torque. No engine hop-up kits are available, but the police options are many and varied, ranging from strengthening in certain areas to different seats to allow comfortable wearing of guns and so on.

Because of the construction of the car, very few have light bars fitted; most rely on concealed lights, so as not to affect the aerodynamics as much as anything.

Some officers have described the Mustang as twitchy, but most agree the performance is superb and most offenders give in quite quickly rather than try and outrun one!

While the Mustang earned its spurs as a muscle car capable of dealing with high speeds and

offenders, its performance and single-mindedness did not make it ideal as a regular patrol car. However, Ford was not worried as it had the Crown Victoria, the company's best selling police car, in service virtually everywhere.

Crown Victoria
There are two types commonly seen on the roads, those made before 1992 and a more aerodynamic version made since then. Thanks to the longevity

of this vehicle, there are still many of the earlier versions in service alongside the newer vehicles.

Interestingly, it was not until after 1992 that a police package was offered for the Crown Victoria. This saw the 302 engine—competent but not a great performer—replaced by a V-8.

The change in motor upped the horsepower from 160 to 210 and gave a top speed just in excess of 120mph. However, it is not figures such as these that make the Crown Victoria so popular;

Left: A Ford Mustang belonging to the Florida Highway Patrol cooling off in the shade in the "Sunshine State."

Above: Georgia State Patrol Mustang showing it is possible to fit a bar light to a Mustang if you are careful!

No matter which way you look at it, the Mustang is a car that looks the part, especially when it wears the livery of the California Highway Patrol. Even stationary it looks like it can run with the best of them, so most don't run!

36

safety considerations feature high on this car's list of attributes.

There are disc brakes on all four wheels, with ABS and traction control as extras. Extra strengthening is used making the Crown Victoria a lot safer in the event of a collision, although much of this work is primarily to cater for the users' demands rather than primarily for safety.

Below: This is an early model Crown Victoria in use with Cook County Sheriff's office parked alongside an identical type of car. Note, however, the different bar light fitments, showing the variations between cars in use by the same agency. *Ken Young*

Below: This post-1992 model shows how much smarter and smoother the Crown Vic has become, seen here in the markings of Kentucky State Police.

Above: A Crown Vic in the colors of the California Highway Patrol complete with a Vision light bar. Once again the black and white livery adds a purposeful look to this post-1992 version.

Right: This Iowa State Patrol officer is standing reflecting on the brand new 1992 model Crown Vic of which he has just taken delivery. This was the first of the new shape models.

Above and Right: The clean lines of the Crown Vic remain the same but the differences in markings and the use of bar lights change the overall appearance of these two examples. *Ken Young (Above)*

Above: Just a change of color and markings make it look almost a different car!

Above: The Mississippi Highway Patrol livery is very similar to the Kansas color scheme even to the yellow of the shield on the door. It could make you lose your bearings!

Right: The Montana Highway Patrol used the Crown Vic as a traffic enforcement car. However, today Montana has no daytime speed limit, so the Crown Vic's role in speed enforcement is diminished. At night the dark paintwork and the low bar light makes the Crown Vic very hard to detect until the lights go on.

Above: Unmarked Illinois State Crown Victoria — only the hidden lights and alley light give the game away.

Above: Three Quarter shot showing sleek lines of the new model.

Right: A Rear view of the car on patrol in heavy traffic - again the sleek lines emphasised.

Above: The year of change: 1992 Crown Vic operated by Louisiana State Police. This is a very distinctive model in that it did not have a grille, nor the reflective strip between the two tail lights.

Right: Minnesota State Police markings emphasize the sleek lines of the Crown Vic.

The Missouri State Highway Patrol tends to use many different color schemes for their cars. Seen here (**Above**) in black is a 1995 Crown Vic with no bar light. Compare this with a similar Missouri car (**Right**) in silver and with bar light.

50

Above: Massachusetts use different color doors, fleet numbers, and bar lights to identify their Crown Vics on the turnpike.

Right: Floral Park New York Police Department changes markings more often than it change its vehicles. Seen here is the very latest color scheme and markings on a Crown Vic in 1998.

Above: The earlier, more angular, Crown Vic gleaming in the New Hampshire sun next to a state trooper's later model.

Right: New Jersey State keeps the markings clean and simple, but nevertheless effective, on this late Crown Vic. They are easily identifiable even though mainly in white.

Right: The California Highway Patrol (thanks to CHiPs) is almost as as well known as the Golden Gate Bridge. Pictured here in the fore-ground is a Crown Vic in CHiP's colors behind which can clearly be seen the bridge's impressive super-structure.

Chicago Police vehicle - capable of standing up to the rigours of the Windy City.

Dodge

Dodge is part of the massive Chrysler corporation, which was, at one time, the major supplier of police specification vehicles. All of that has changed: today the only vehicle Dodge offers is under the Jeep name, although the plant in Mexico makes some specials to cope with local problems south of the border!

In the past Dodge produced police specials under both the Dodge and Plymouth brand names, but the last of these came out in 1989 as the Plymouth Fury and Dodge Diplomat. It was in 1956 that the company released its first Mopar police car based on the Cornet with a V-8 motor; it was joined a year later by Plymouth's own versions.

By 1960 Dodge dominated the tests conducted by police authorities to ascertain which were the most suitable cars for police use. More importantly, the end user—i.e. the patrolman—was a big fan of the large Dodges!

Then came the 880 and the Polara, and by the mid-1960s Dodge and Plymouth had taken most of Ford's sales away, with an estimated eight out of every ten police cars wearing the Dodge or Plymouth badge.

But at the turn of the 1970s, emission controls effectively crippled the big motors and cars such as the Dodge Cornet lost a lot of its get up and go. However, as technology came to grips with tighter controls things improved and by the mid-1970s the Dodge Dart and Aspen appeared with just as powerful motors as before.

There was also the Diplomat range of vehicles (featured on pages 60 to 63), but these were not so popular with officers. From the end of the 1970s through the early 1990s, Chrysler had highs and lows and the result is that today the company has just the Jeep Cherokee on offer as a specific police vehicle.

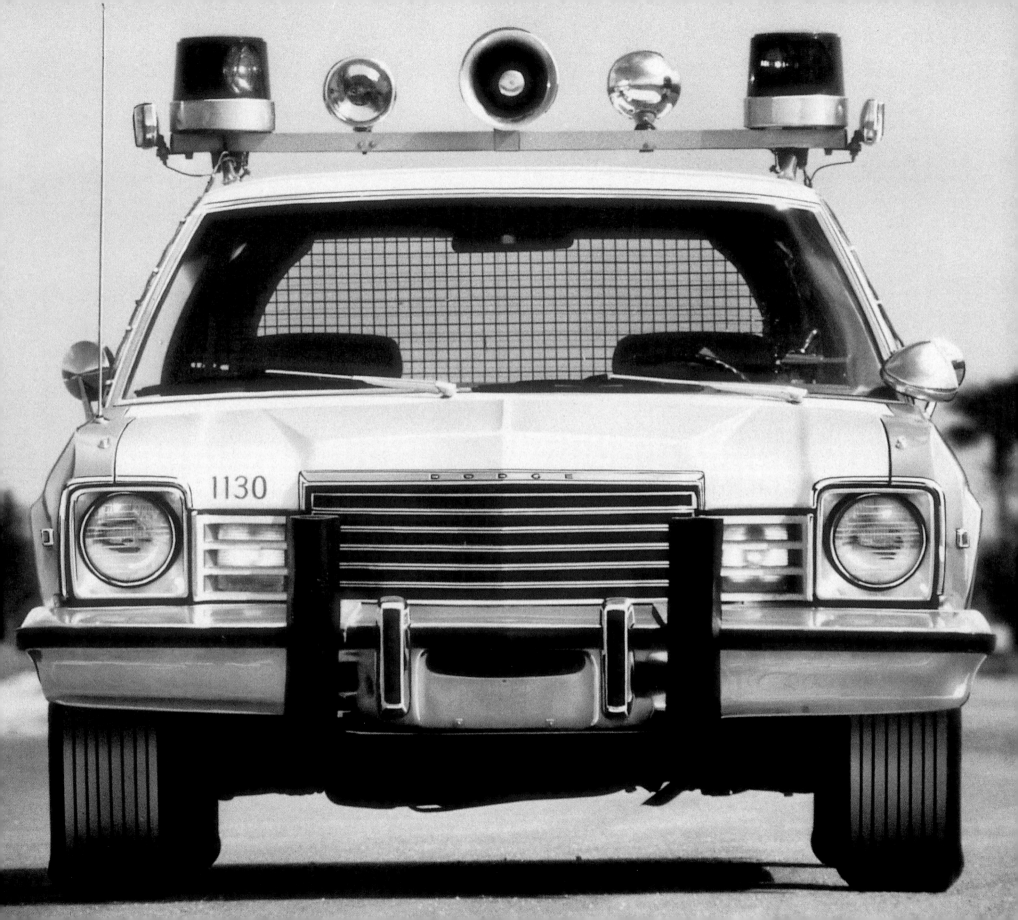

Above: Dodge's only offering to today's police market is the Jeep Cherokee, a 4 x 4 utility vehicle. this is a police dog vehicle from Matteson Village, IL. *Ken Young*

Right: A sorry looking Plymouth Gran Fury seeing out its last days as an Auxiliary Vehicle. *Ken Young*

Chevrolet

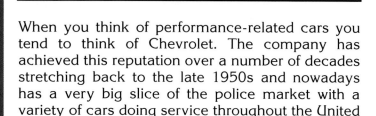

When you think of performance-related cars you tend to think of Chevrolet. The company has achieved this reputation over a number of decades stretching back to the late 1950s and nowadays has a very big slice of the police market with a variety of cars doing service throughout the United States.

Caprice

The Chevrolet Caprice comes in two basic body shapes, those made before 1990 and those after. The difference is very obvious and easy to spot,

with the earlier vehicle having a very square appearance and the later versions very smooth rounded lines. Quite a lot of the earlier versions are still doing service today, such was the standard and quality of the car.

It was offered with a choice of two engines, a small block V-8 and a V-6, both with automatic transmission and with lock-up torque converters and an overdrive. There was little in the top speed between the two versions, it was just the acceleration that differed greatly. Numerous options as to the actual specification were offered, relating to strengthening of body areas, wiring options, and so on.

The new vehicles' sleekly flowing lines were a great improvement on the earlier, more boxy, shape. An additional benefit was that the first of the

Below: This pre-1990 Caprice is still doing service with Floral Park Police although its duties mainly revolve around parking enforcement.

Below Right: An early Caprice in use with Illinois State Police. Although showing out as a police vehicle when close, from a distance it is hard to spot, especially in the rear view mirror! *Ken Young*

Far Right: A pre-1990 Caprice alongside a Chevrolet pick-up truck used by Alaska state troopers; in front their drivers wear different uniforms.

Below: One of the last of the early Caprices awaiting the fitting of a light bar in 1990. You can see the wiring is already in place to connect up the light.

Right: This late Caprice shows the markings of the Beverley Hills State.

new-shaped cars achieved higher top speeds with the previous engine and drivetrain fitted. However, at first drivers did not like it as much as the earlier version. This was mainly because the flowing lines meant drivers could not see all four corners of the car from the driving seat, especially the front end. As with most things, they came to terms with it and the Caprice has risen to become one of the best-selling police cars.

Like its predecessor it comes with two engine options but this time both are small-block V-8s. The smaller unit—the 305—has a 170hp rating and is intended for town use. The larger 350 gives 205bhp and is intended for open road use. This has the advantage of allowing a fleet to be standardized apart from engine parts!

A host of police options are available and in 1994 Chevrolet even offered a larger 26bhp motor making the Caprice one of the fastest four-door sedan police cars ever made.

Below: A fully kitted Maryland State Police Caprice sheltering behind the brickwork ready for action.

Right: A more soberly attired Caprice from Virginia showing the neatly integrated flowing lines of the car's rear.

Above: Looking mean and menacing, these all-black Caprices belong to New York State.

Right: A Caprice in the black and white livery of West Virginia State Police complete with a boot-mounted spoiler, not a standard fitment in many other states.

Above: Although Floral Park may run a few older ones, this post-1990 model Caprice has the Corvette engine fitted, just in case somebody decides to make a run for it!

Right: North Carolina uses a two-tone paint job with a low-level light bar on this late Caprice.

Right and Below: Two variations on a basic theme. Although wearing the same paint job, these two Caprices in New Hampshire differ in that one has no light bar, showing how things vary in the same police department. It could well show a difference in engine size.

Far Right: Two-tone paint and side markings are the order of the day in the Tennessee Highway Patrol, seen here sitting in the shade.

Above: A late Caprice used for supervision, but fully kitted and ready to go. You can clearly see all the information displayed on the vehicle, along with the multi-colored bar light. *Ken Young*

Right: In black and white trim and fully kitted this Caprice sits ready for action.

Above: No doubt most police departments would love to double their fleet and manpower so easily. Reflected in a Washington puddle this Caprice is as immaculate as the officer. Note the addition of nudge bars at the front.

Right: Hidden lights in the grille are the key point on this shot of a Maine State Police Caprice.

Above: Arkansas extend the blue line across the bonnet to show in a rear-view mirror and have a low-level bar light on their late model Caprice.

Right: Wearing the new markings of the Arizona State Patrol, this Caprice is ready for action.

Below: This Camaro was seized in Ohio as part of a drugs bust. It is an early model with a light bar and crest and is now earning its keep legally!

Right: Idaho has one as well but with no bar light and in black and white livery!

Camaro

There was no way that Chevrolet was ever going to let Ford have its own way and be the only supplier of high performance vehicles to the police. The Camaro, therefore, was the company's response to the Ford Mustang.

Launched as a police special in 1991 with two engine options and the option of manual or automatic gearbox, it had one aim—to deal with traffic violators. Top speed is one thing—and the Camaro came in with a blistering 152mph in tests—but it was the way it accelerated that attracted the interest.

A car that has to chase another from a stationary position or after turning round needs to be capable of good acceleration. The Camaro can out-accelerate most things—including the Mustang. This means a speeding vehicle can be caught quickly, so people tend not to try outrunning it; it's also a great police recruitment tool!

Despite being drop-dead gorgeous, the car was redesigned in 1993 to look even better and the Corvette engine was fitted, giving 275bhp.

The usual host of police options was on offer as usual. What better way to earn a living?

Above: New York State Police have a mean looking black Camaro complete with bar light.

Right: These three red Camaros were part of a an illegal property seizure in Ohio. Rather than let them go to waste they added a crest to the doors and a light bar to the roof before putting them to work as part of their Highway Patrol fleet!

Optional Extras

Below Right: A shield, normally the same as that worn by the officers, is often emblazoned on the front doors to identify the police authority that operates the vehicle.

Far Right: The famous black and white color scheme on a Beverley Hills patrol car!

To a certain extent most police vehicles look exactly the same as those anyone can buy at a car dealership. What sets them aside is the alterations beneath the bodywork, such as the modification of steering, suspension, and engine changes to allow them to cope with the rigors of the job they are expected to do on a daily basis.

One of the major differences is in the electrical department. Alterations are made to allow additional equipment to be run without interfering with engine management systems, or flattening the battery due to increased loading. Then, of course, there are changes to door locking systems, etc.

These are not the most visible differences; the

Below: Another location for the shield, as demonstrated by the NYPD.

Right: Uniformity of both vehicle and officer is demonstrated by the Idaho State police, making both readily identifiable as part of the law enforcement team. *Archive Photos*

ones the public see are the visual changes—the addition of bar lights, warning lights hidden in the grille, alley lights for seeking out fleeing suspects, and, of course, markings.

These may be as elaborate as complete vehicle color schemes, or they may be as simple as just the addition of a crest or badge to a door. These days markings have also to be applied to the roof to allow helicopters to identify vehicles from the air, especially when several are involved.

Recognition

Except for undercover or covert cars, a police patrol vehicle needs to be capable of being identified—the most obvious reason being that a speeding motorist is not going to stop for any vehicle that just wants to flag them down.

To this end, even the most sparsely marked vehicle has a door shield that identifies the agency or department to which it belongs. Failing this, the actual word "Police" is used, normally in large

This side shot of a New York patrol car clearly shows how a plain color scheme can be used to good effect. There is the shield and police lettering; the word police in case anyone is left in any doubt, and the motto is on the rear door.

This is a supervisor's vehicle, although a fleet or identification number is still used, and is repeated across the boot for air identification purposes. This vehicle also shows which precinct it comes from!

Below: Typical NYPD markings.

Right: The word "Police" emblazoned across the bonnet certainly aids identification in the rear-view mirror.

letters along the side of the vehicle, or possibly "Sheriff" or "Highway Patrol."

Rear markings include "911," relating to the emergency phone number, or a local identifying number to allow people to differentiate between one vehicle and another. Supervisors' vehicles may also be marked up on the sides and nowadays what paintwork is left is sometimes filled with slogans! The roof gets air identification marks according to local needs, but each is unique to the particular vehicle.

In addition to actual words, reflective tape is

Below: Slogans now quite often appear in any space left after official recognition markings.

Right: Still New York but a blue and white livery

used in a similar fashion to European police cars, to ensure the vehicle stand outs not just during the day but also at night time. Tape is not only quicker to apply and remove when the vehicle is eventually sold on from police service, but also means it is cheaper to repair in the event of an accident.

Flashing lights
There was a time when just a single red light, rotating through 360 degrees on the top of the vehicle,

was used. The first were seen in the late 1940s and had a substantial aerodynamic drag. However, as cars have evolved and become more aerodynamic, so the lights have had to blend in with the flowing lines of the vehicle. Lights now normally consist of light bars that are lower and sleeker than the originals; despite all this, the new lights give a 7% drag, which is still more than the original single rotating light unit!

The advantage of a light bar, however, is that all

Police and Community Together

Below: Numbers can also go over the trunk lid for air recognition purposes, as the close-up clearly shows. This is particularly necessary when a bar light may cut down on the lettering sizes.

Right: Whatever the color scheme, the numbers are big and bold!

Right: A police patrol car rushing to an incident with his single rotating red roof light in operation. Not the most effective item against the bright lights of night-time New York City and one of the reasons for change!

Above: Same place different time, but still at night. An early light bar, but coupled with the newer markings on the vehicle it is easier to spot the police vehicle against the reduced light available.

Above: A relatively basic bar light with red one side, blue the other. Note the white center area for illumination when stopping a vehicle at night time.

Right: A more complex unit that has amber lights incorporated.

U.S. PAT. 4,543,622 286,756 CAN. PAT. 54,314   PUBLIC SAFETY EQUIPMENT, INC.   ST. LOUIS, MO. 63146 USA   SAE-W3-83

FORCE 4® LP

ARROWSTIK

DISCONNECT POWER BEFORE SERVICING
TO CHANGE BULBS. SLIDE CIRCUIT BOARD
ASSEMBLY OUT FROM CABLE END
DO NOT REMOVE LENS
REPLACE BULBS WITH TYPE 211-2

CODE 3
PUBLIC SAFETY EQUIPMENT

Right: This light bar still has the basic four colors of red, blue, amber, and white but giving a greater variation on the way that they can be used either on the move or when stationary at an incident

Above: No matter how many colors it uses front and back, the side of a bar light normally has two powerful white lights that can be used to illuminate alleys and dark areas as the car passes slowly by—hence the term "alley lights." These are fixed and have no movement available.

Below: Red lights are good by day, less so by night.

Right: Lights like these have to be shielded from a driver when front mounted to prevent flashes bouncing back and taking attention from the road.

the various light colors are covered in one unit, from warning lights to alley lights on the sides. Light bars are quick and easy to fit, and only need one power and operation source. They are more powerful in terms of intensity and frequency of flashes, or pulses in the case of strobe lights.

Research showed that, although the traditional red light was visible during daylight hours, at night blue was an easier color for the eye to recognize, so most bars incorporate both these primary colors.

While white lights are used at the side to illuminate buildings or alleys, they are also used at the front to light up a suspect's vehicle while the officer approaches. These are commonly called "take down" lights. The different combinations used by agencies are so varied you could almost write a book on these alone; some even include a matrix that gives commands to following traffic. Some also have a siren loudspeaker in the center to project sound further above the line of traffic.

Left: The addition of airbags to vehicles meant driver operated alley lights had to be repositioned so as not to impede airbag deployment.

Left and Far Left: Close-up of manually operated "alley lights" that can be moved from inside the car by the driver or passenger. The driver's is normally white. They are operated by hand and have a greater degree of flexibility than roof-mounted items.

Below Right: While radios were quite common in the 1940s, they were still bulky items and very basic. This officer shows that the handset was little more than an adapted telephone handset!

Far Right: This shot of a current patrol car shows how small and compact a modern radio is. Mounted at the bottom between the front two seats with a small neat handset, this will use many different frequencies. Above it, in the middle, are the screens and key pad for the mobile data terminal, and just above this is the bar light control panel, incorporating the sirens. The handset is for the PA system incorporated within it to allow public service broadcasts as well as commands for suspect vehicles, etc.

While most police cars have some form of roof-mounted light, many agencies still feel they affect adversely vehicle stability and handling. Because of this, lights mounted inside the vehicle behind the windshield or inset into the front radiator grille are preferred.

Whilst on the subject of lights, there are also the "alley-lights" mounted on the A post and operated from within by a long pistol-grip handle. These can be used through all sorts of angles and are more useful in some situations than those fixed beams on the side of the light bars. Recent advances in vehicle safety, such as the air bag, have caused a problem in fitting these so they do not affect the deployment of the bag.

Sirens
While the lights assault the visual senses, the electric sirens attract attention by intruding into even the loudest of in-car entertainment systems. These

BAR LIGHT CONTROL PANEL

HANDSET FOR PA SYSTEM

SCREEN AND KEYPAD

MOBILE DATA TERMINAL

RADIO

HANDSET

Below Right: Night use of these systems gives the appearance of a mobile electricity substation, hence the need for alterations to the vehicles electrical systems if an officer is not to be stranded with a flat battery at night!

Far Right: A state trooper makes good use of his clip board to write a ticket for a traffic violation

modern units replaced the old bells and are capable of varying tone and pitch as well as volume, to give audible warning of approach.

Most of these units incorporate a loudspeaker system to allow vehicle occupants to make public addresses or give commands to suspects. This allows an officer to remain inside his vehicle until he is sure it is safe to get out and approach a suspect's vehicle. These systems can be wired to operate from the horn or can be used independently.

Radios

The old style radios were large, heavy, and cumbersome; the new ones allow a multitude of frequencies and channels to be covered from just a small, compact, control unit in the front of the vehicle. Some patrol vehicles also have CB radios fitted to help motorists, as well as to call on their assistance at times!

Some radios act as a base station allowing the officer to use the main radio via a repeater set when he leaves the vehicle, adding to officer safety.

Below: Windows in the rear of vehicles used to carry prisoners are often adapted to prevent them opening all the way or sufficiently for somebody to squeeze through!

Other additions.

While the previously mentioned items—lights, sirens, radios, etc.—are standard fare, other additional equipment varies considerably depending on the agency concerned. Some are now fitting mobile data terminals (MDTs), allowing the officer on the street to conduct his own checks directly without going through a base station. All sorts of data can be accessed, from licence plates, to advice on hazardous materials, as well as checks on individuals.

Radar is another item frequently carried, especially by highway patrol vehicles. Most systems are hand-held items operating on the K-Band.

Somewhere on the inside of a police car will normally be found a range of weapons to protect the officer, along with flashlights, clip boards, and relevant paperwork such as traffic tickets.

Left: A solid grille is often put between the front and rear of the vehicle to allow it to carry prisoners whilst maintaining the driver's safety. The normal rear seats are removed and replaced with a fibreglass item with scallops cut for the arms, elbows, and cuffed hands. There is a three-point fixing belt to hold the prisoner in place. Solid rubber matting on the floor assists in preventing a prisoner from stashing illegal drugs or stolen property. Although door handles remain, the actual doors can only be opened from outside the vehicle.

Above: Even the roof is used for mounting speed detection equipment. Note also the large interior light to allow paper-work to be completed.

Above: Once again the roof being used to carry equiment, this time for the protection of the vehicle's occupants.

Left: This shot clearly shows the pistol grip operation of the driver's alley light mounted through the A-pillar.

Below: Two unmarked cars. While no markings are displayed but you can clearly see here the concealed lights. However, until they are lit (when it is too late!) they are not visible on the state highway. *Ken Young (Both)*

The boot will not normally have a lot of room left compared to a civilian car thanks to radio controllers, strobe units etc. However, what space is left will be taken up with first aid kits, spare tires, gas, auxiliary weapons, restraints, and personal equipment such as jackets and waterproofs.

As you can see the car is very much a place of work and a tool to do a job getting the law enforcement officer to a location as quickly and as safely as possible!

Above: Viewed from the passenger side the driving compartment looks even more like an office with space becoming even more limited as technological aids are added.

Above: Chevrolet Camaro used for high speed pursuits by the police department in Idaho. The bar light making it more visible on general patrol.

Right: No visible lights on this Idaho Chevrolet Camaro, whose side markings have been extended across the front of the vehicle making it easier to identify in the mirror.

Above: A more conventionally marked 1992 Ford Crown Victoria in service with the Missouri State Patrol. The plain white color is broken only by the shield on the door and the words "State Trooper" on the front wings. A low light bar completes the marking.

Right: A state trooper from Vermont showing a basic single blue rotating light on his Plymouth Gran Fury.

Right: Beverly Hills markings clearly stand out on a plain door.

Far Right: A 1992 Ford Crown Victoria of the same make and model, but different use of markings and lights change the whole appearance of the car *Ken Young*.

Above: A 1993 Crown Victoria in service with Georgia State Police. Here the vehicle's paint scheme helps identify the vehicle as well as the bold lettering down the sides. (Note this vehicle has smaller hub caps as the larger ones have tended to come off and act as Frisbees during pursuits!)

Right: A Chevrolet Caprice using reflective stripes to help identify the vehicle. Note the door shield is very large and the word "Police" has got a lot smaller.

Right: Pennsylvania State Police Chevrolet Caprice with a Vision lightbar. Note how this consists of individual lights mounted on a single angled metal bar across the vehicle.

Below: New York State Ford Mustang with an all-red light bar apart from pull down white lights in the center.

Right: A Nebraska State patrol officer sits in his Ford Mustang awaiting speeding motorists. This is a typical angled approach adopted by a vehicle while the driver uses a hand-held radar. It is at an angle to give the gun a chance to catch the speeding vehicle within the spread of its beam.

Above: A Chevrolet Caprice in Oklahoma relying mainly on its color scheme to identify it as a law enforcement vehicle until the hidden lights are switched on!

Right: The end result of a chase: the driver of a speeding vehicle receives a citation for his trouble. Note the various colors on this light bar fitted to the Texas Trooper's Camaro.

130

Above and Right: These reflect reflect the range of police cars in service throughout the United States. Top—Downers Grove, IL, Chevrolet 2500 used as a scenes of crime vehicle; Above—Ford Explorer of Bannockburn Police; Above Right—Federal Protection Service ford Explorer; Below Right—NSWC pick-up. *Ken Young (All)*

132

Below: A Camero in a more traditional black and white scheme with a multi-colored light bar showing how much easier it is to spot both from the side and in a mirror. It also looks more aggressive in these colors!

Above: European vehicles have made only rare inroads into the police forces of the United States — here, a Series 3 BMW of the Georgia State Patrol.0

Above: Pre-1990 Chevrolet Caprice in use with the California Highway Patrol; note a set of bars at the front can clearly be seen These have a role in protecting the radiator and lights if the car is used to nudge a suspect vehicle. They also give it the capability to push a broken-down vehicle off the highway without causing damage and is an example as to how individual agencies adapt the standard police package to suit their own needs.

Right: A 1992 Crown Victoria in use in Ohio with additional information on the back doors of the vehicle.

136

Above: A traditional black and white colour scheme for this fully kitted Beverly Hills patrol vehicle.

Above: Four different markings showing the range of colors and messages used. *Ken Young (All)*

Right: No matter how good the car it still needs a driver. This New York officer seems happy enough with his chosen vehicle.

Far Right: An unusual sight — a foreign vehicle in use. This Series 3 BMW serves with the Georgia State Patrol. Its somber marking scheme will make it hard to spot, especially with the blue paintwork masking the bar light colors. *Ken Young*

Below: A pre-1991 Ford Crown Victoria used by California Highway Patrol. As with many vehicles in use with CHP, this has only a red spotlight on the driver's side and a red light behind the rear-view mirror. Note also the nudge bars at the front.

Right: Despite Delaware State troopers posing proudly next to the helicopter providing air support, they have no roof markings on the Ford Crown Victoria to help the pilot identify individual cars!

Right: This photograph dates back to the days when Connecticut troopers removed the light bar when going off duty, allowing them private use of the car. This Ford Crown Victoria just has the words "State Police" between the red and blue lights on the bar, and no other distinguishing marks!

Specialist Vehicles

Right, Far Right, and Overleaf: Although these three cars all look different, they all perform the same basic function—that of a patrol vehicle responding to calls. They have limited equipment on board and their carrying capacity of officers is likely to be only two persons. They will, however, be fast and on arrival at an incident be in a position to make an assessment and call out the specialized vehicles and equipment needed to deal with the situation in the most effective manner.

While the car makes up the bulk of any police fleet, it is not capable of performing all motorized transport tasks. For instance, in very congested areas it is not capable of making progress through heavy traffic. It is not fuel efficient or environmentally friendly in such situations either, especially with only one officer on board. It is also not capable of carrying heavy loads or specialized equipment to the scene of major incidents. Lastly, its carrying capacity of personnel is also limited.

To get around these problems, specialized vehicles are used. These will not necessarily patrol in the same way as a car, but sit in readiness to be

Right: Small three-wheelers such as this Cushman are quite a common sight with public utilities, the police are no exception. Shown is one in service with the NYPD used for traffic duties.

called out as and when their specialized equipment or capability is needed. There's a long list of these vehicles on the strength of all police forces including snowmobiles, quad-bikes, off-road vehicles, even tanks and diggers such is the diversity of police activities these days!

There are so many variations and adaptations of

vehicles that it is impossible to cover all of them in this book. Indeed, many would look just like an ordinary car or van from the outside, especially when we are talking about surveillance vehicles. This section gives a flavor of a few of the more mainstream specialist vehicles in use on a day-to-day basis.

Right: The first form of mobile patrol—the horse. Nowadays not suitable for covering long distances, but still useful in cities both for general patrol duties and in crowd control situations. There are not many who wish to argue with a ton of horse pounding towards them!

Below Right: Not all two-wheeled mounts are large-capacity motorcycles. Shown here are two officers on patrol in New York on their scooters in 1970. The leg shields and large screen give good weather protection and the small lightweight machines are very nippy through traffic—top speed in cities is not an issue. Note also that these still display ID numbers like the cars. *Archive Photos*

Far Right: Probably one of the cheapest patrol vehicles is the pedal cycle. Again very useful in towns and cities and also in areas where vehicles are prohibited, they allow an officer to patrol a far greater area than on foot and also have the added advantage of maintaining fitness. It also means the officer is more readily available to the public rather than being enclosed in a vehicle which needs to be flagged down!

Above: This photograph dates to the mid-1970s when Harley were the only surviving U.S. motorcycle producer, under pressure from the Japanese who are manufacturing police specials for highway patrols. Seen here is a motorcycle patrolman in Washington D.C. on a large capacity Harley-Davidson police bike. *Lambert/Archive Photos*

Right: Into the 1990s and Harleys are still there with the bulk of the police market. This New York Harley may be marked differently and have a different light configuration, but it is basically the same bike that was on patrol in Washington D.C.—a timeless classic that can still do the job despite the pressure from the east!

Right: Pressure from the east comes in the form of the Kawasaki 1000P.

Far Right: An unmarked police vehicle that can still be identified by the lights mounted either side on the A posts. Not all unmarked police vehicles are this easy to spot as they use a magnetic light when they want to make progress through traffic.

Top: Staying with four legs— the horse box. These carry several horses at a time and allow them to arrive close to their destination fresh and ready to go. Although no more special than an ordinary horsebox it still wears police livery.

Below: One of the specialist vehicles that goes out on patrol—the K9 vehicle complete with its occupants. Although in the past these have been, and in some cases still are, adapted saloons, there is now a move to estates and four-wheel drive vehicles to carry the dogs. These have to have adaptations such as ventilation and cages, to allow their canine occupants to travel in comfort and safety.

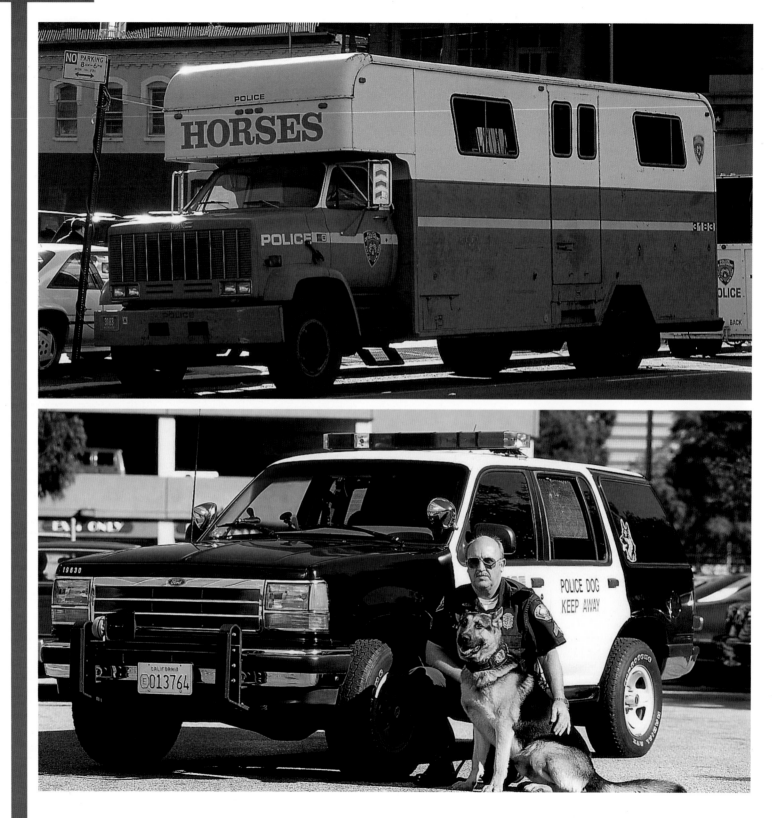

Left and Below: Two views of an estate or shooting brake used by the NYPD as a bomb squad vehicle. Its carrying capacity allows them to carry their specialized equipment, but still be faster and more maneuverable than a van. They are marked to provide a high visible presence on the streets.

Right and Below Right: Truck used to carry a variety of equipment for rescue purposes; it is capable of carrying heavyweight items all stowed in the back and easily accessed at the scene of an incident.

Left: A parked Sheboygan van in use in 1977 for prisoner transport. *Riegler/Archive Photos*

Below: A more modern use of a van as a Crime Scene Unit. This will have all the equipment needed to investigate a crime. It is not a general patrol vehicle but one that goes out as required hence its few markings; it is, however, easily identifiable at a scene. Note ladders on top ready to deal with any eventuality!

The end of the line when it all goes wrong! *The Image Bank*